THE HISTORY

LIVERPOOL

JEWISH COMMUNITY.

Re-printed from the "Jewish World," August, 1877.

London :

PRINTED AT THE OFFICES OF THE "JEWISH WORLD,"

8, South Street, Finsbury, E.C.

THE HISTORY OF THE LIVERPOOL JEWISH COMMUNITY.

THERE is something very unromantic in the origin of most of our Anglo-Jewish communities. Unlike those of Italy, Holland and the Rhine, which were founded by martyrs, exiles, and those who had suffered and bled for their faith, there is a kind of monotony in the early history of our English provincial communities. First there comes a substratum of poor Germans or Poles, who pioneer the way into a town as hawkers, pedlars, or watchmakers ; then commences the struggle for livelihood and the desire to educate their offspring in the religious faith of their ancestors ; and lastly, there arrives a superior stratum of new comers, who help to fertilise the soil that has been cleared and prepared by the original humble settlers. The history of the Jewish congregations in Liverpool does not take the writer back to a very remote period. When it is considered that this gigantic port was at the commencement of the present century little better than a small fishing town, of under twenty thousand inhabitants, it can be readily understood that there were then no especial attractions for the settlement of our coreligionists.

It is well for this large and flourishing Jewish community in Liverpool that the financial and mercantile interests of the borough have necessitated, of late years, the residence in Liverpool of educated and influential coreligionists, otherwise it would have shared the fate of such congregations as Falmouth, Norwich, and Yarmouth ; for few of the decendants of the first humble settlers remain, and the actual born Jewish Liverpudlians are the small minority.

The advent of Jews to the great emporium of Lancashire took place about the end of the last century, and the immigrants consisted of persons engaged in vending " clothes, watches, and jewellery," to the seafaring population. The early Jewish inhabitants were Germans and Poles, and with their characteristic zeal for the religious observances of their forefathers, they soon assembled for religious worship in a small house in Turton Court, near the Custom House, in 1780. The early records of the congregation which are still in existence, were kept in the Hebrew-German jargon ; they bear the date of 5560, exactly 78 years ago, are very interesting, and give a vivid picture of the social standing of these first residents. Law 6 contains the following interesting paragraph in "Jüdisch-Deutsch:" "None of our congregation who receive a summons to be called to the Law dare wear jack-boots outside his trousers, nor a coloured handkerchief round his neck, nor may he chew tobacco. Should he commit any of these acts he will be fined a shilling." A previous law states that no member called to the Torah on the holidays dare *schnoder* less than sixpence.

A few years later a more ambitious move took place; a small freehold house, with garden attached, in Frederick Street, was acquired, which they used as a synagogue and a cemetery. This house is still the property of the old Hebrew Congregation, and used as a "Mickvah," or bath. The cemetery is in a wretched and woe-begone condition, and does not reflect credit upon the surviving descendants of those interred there. Among the first who assisted in Divine service was one Rev. B. Goetz: the relations have since adopted the name of "Yates" instead of Goetz. He seems to have been what is almost a necessity in small communities—a *multum in parvo*—being Mohel, Schochet, Chazan, Secretary, and Collector, at the same time carrying on his calling of engraver and working jeweller. His daughter, a centenarian, a Mrs. Chapman, is still living in Liverpool. The gradual increase of the Jews, and the desire for affording accommodation for the opposite sex (the Frederick Street Synagogue having no gallery for ladies), made it imperative to further enlarge the room for public worship. In 1807 the Seel Street Synagogue was erected—a neat but unpretending edifice, which, until 1874, when the magnificent new synagogue in Prince's Road was consecrated (of which we shall treat later on) served to supply all the spiritual requirements of the Jews until a lamentable schism took place.

In the Seel Street Synagogue the first sermons ever preached by Jews in the English language were delivered soon after the consecration by Mr. Tobias Goodman and Mr. Nathan, brother of the Rev. M. N. Nathan, formerly of St. Thomas', but now a resident in London. The Rev. Professor Marks, minister of the Berkeley Street Congregation, was also attached to this synagogue in his youthful days, and gave early promise of that talent which he has since so largely developed. The Rev. Professor D. M. Isaacs, at present in Manchester, was the first regularly appointed English preacher, and attracted large congregations by his eloquence and his earnest zeal in all religious matters. Another cemetery was purchased in the early part of this century in the London Road, which was then a rural district, but is now thickly inhabited and in the very midst of busy streets. This was closed in 1835, and the present one in Deane Road consecrated. This ground is very ornamental, beautifully laid out, and well kept, and a pleasant contrast to the original burying place of the first Jewish settlers. It seems, however, the fate of the new cemetery, like its predecessors, to be swallowed up by the inevitable march of brick and stucco, which has transformed the district from a green meadow into a flourishing suburb covered with endless terraces and genteel semi-detached villas. The entrance to the ground is graced by a very chaste portico in pure classic style of architecture, and bearing upon the pediment the verse, " Here the weary are at rest." About this period there seems to have been the commencement of a series of differences in the community, which culminated in an angry secession of more than half the congregation; and although the breach has been healed by the gentle hand of Time, it will take another generation to efface entirely all traces of the bitter feeling engendered by the separation.

To enter into the causes of the quarrel would necessitate more space than this journal could afford, but from a pamphlet printed in 1838, containing an address by Mr. B. L. Joseph and a report of a public meeting of the Jews, held in the Clarendon Rooms, on 1st October of that year, it seems that the seceders were anxious for peace, but that the then existing authorities of the Seel Street Congregation, by the tyranny which small country communities knew how to wield in those days, left them no option but to retire.

It seems that the minority of privileged members, fearing the large ingress of strangers might detract somewhat from their assumed importance, blackballed every applicant for free membership or levied a prohibitory fee of admission of £27 5s. When it is considered that at that date the entire income from seat-rental amounted to £287, it will be seen how unwise, to say the least, this imposition was. In short, the small minority desired to tax and rule the vast majority, without giving the latter any voice in their deliberations. All efforts to bring the ruling powers to a sense of justice being unavailing, the seceding body opened a small synagogue in Hardman Street, and in 1842, their members having largely increased, they erected a very elegant place of worship in Hope Place, wherein the new congregation now worship. To add to the disorder in the Seel Street Synagogue, the Rev. Professor Isaacs having addressed to the congregation some plain truths, perhaps unpalatable to the oligarchical rulers, caused the transfer of that talented preacher to the new congregation.

But the evil was not without its corresponding good. Utter ruin staring the elder congregation in the face, they immediately, upon the opening of the Hope Place Synagogue, reduced their fee for free membership to one guinea, became more conciliatory, endeavoured to cultivate a better feeling with the seceders, and by so doing the prestige and repute which attached to the older body soon restored its position as a leading community with a guiding influence in Jewish matters.

Some idea of the feeling existing amongst the Jews in Liverpool at that period will be evidenced by an extract from some stanzas printed in a Jewish publication called the " Cup of Salvation," which was edited by the Rev. Professor Isaacs and the late Moses Samuel, (a Liverpool resident of superior attainments). The poem bears the initials " E. L. S." It will not be difficult to trace the author. He writes :—

> " 'Tis sad to see our hallowed creed
>   By ignorance descried,
> The faith for which our hearts would bleed,
>   Fell prejudice deride.
>
> But sadder far 'tis to behold,
>   The men who should protect,
> The members of the Jewish fold,
>   Conspiring 'gainst their sect.
>
> Whose hearts to pity's promptings dead—
>   No patriot flame can feel ;
> The germs of dire dissension spread,
>   Regardless of our weal."

It is far more pleasant now to narrate the gradual advance and development of both congregations and their combined efforts for the educational and social improvement of their members, and especially of their poorer brethren.

A school, originally planned by the very earnest and talented Mr. Abraham, a relative of our distinguished co-religionist, Mr. Serjeant Simon, M.P., and aided by the munificence of the late Israel Barned, a wealthy banker in the town, was erected in Hope Place, adjoining the new synagogue. This was opened by the Rev. the Chief Rabbi in 1852, and now gives elementary education to about 300 children.

We shall now proceed with the fuller history of the Old Hebrew Congregation.

The losses incurred by the secession of the new congregation having been fully made up by the influx into the town of gentlemen holding important and influential positions in the mercantile world, gave a very superior tone to the elder synagogue. The new blood that had been infused soon made itself felt in a very marked manner. Dr. Fischel was elected lecturer, who, having obtained an appointment in New York, was succeeded by Dr. Baar, a clergyman of highly refined manner and of superior culture, and whose influence was salutary in the highest degree. The old congregation were equally fortunate in their minister and reader, the Rev. Professor Prag being one of the most learned Hebrew scholars in Great Britain, whilst their secretary, the Reverend R. Harris, now of the Bayswater Synagogue, also added to the excellence of the congregational management; and a very superior choir, led by Mr. A. Saqui, enhanced the attractiveness of the Divine worship, and made the service of the Seel Street Synagogue one worthy of imitation by all other Jewish communities. After the translation of the Rev. R. Harris to London, a most efficient secretary, Mr. H. M. Silver, succeeded him, and by his admirable tact, his excellent skill in organisation, has not a little helped the rapid advancement of the community; indeed, there is hardly an institution in the town, whether it be the schools, the Board of Guardians, or the Anglo-Jewish Association, that is not enriched by his vast experience in secretarial duties. A small reaction commenced in the prosperity of the synagogue by the unfortunate retirement of Dr. Baar, owing to the entire loss of his voice. The synagogue began to lose many worshippers, and a languor seemed to creep upon the actions of the executive. It was difficult to obtain wardens, many having preferred to pay fines rather than take their share in the communal government, and the committees were attenuated and lax in their attendance, when a new era of prosperity dawned by the election of Mr. A. Hoffnung as president of the community. It is true there were great men before Agamemnon, but to be universally beloved and to inspire confidence and zealous co-operation in others is the lot of but a few. This is what Mr. Hoffnung had done; he not only led himself in every good work, but induced others in whom he perceived the existence of talent to work with him. In Mr. Augustus S. Levy, Mr. B. L. Benas, Mr. L. S. Cohen, and Mr. S. Y. Hess he found coadjutors that enabled them to achieve such results that had never been attained by any provincial body, and it may be doubted whether ever any Jewish community in the metropolis has accomplished so much. What Mr. Hoffnung particularly taught the Jews of Liverpool was to have faith in their own capabilities, and that the energies of each and every section of the community might be utilised and applied for a beneficial purpose. When it was decided to erect another sacred edifice in lieu of the one in Seel Street, it was barely expected that £3,000 could be raised, and the project flagged, until Mr. Hoffnung took the matter decisively in hand. It was then that the entire sum of £12,722 was collected, and the most beautiful Jewish temple in England was consecrated, entirely free from debt, and without any appeal beyond the town itself. Of this amount £3,000 was realised by the Hebrew Ladies' Bazaar, the carrying out of which was hotly opposed by several of the older residents ; indeed, they withdrew themselves entirely from the project, leaving the complete onus and responsibility to the few gentlemen before named ; but, led as they were by Mr. Hoffnung, who was the life and soul of the enterprise, they achieved one of the most marvellous successes, and during the three days the bazaar was open in St. George's Hall, it was thronged by persons of all denominations, the gross sum realised being £3,700 ; whilst the moral influence of the Jews in the town was raised in an incalculable degree.

The synagogue was formally consecrated on September 3rd, 1874, by the Rev. Dr. Adler, the seat rent alone amounting to £1,600, a vivid contrast to £287, the sum contributed in 1838. The Rev. Morris Joseph, formerly of the North London Synagogue, was elected preacher, and has since delivered, weekly, a series of highly instructive and able sermons.

At the conclusion of the work the general body of the Jews assembled and subscribed a sum of £400 for the purchase of a testimonial to Mr. A. Hoffnung, who, having served four years successively as President, refused re-election. This was tendered in the name of the Jewish community, by Mr. Augustus Levy and Mr. B. L. Benas ; but Mr. Hoffnung, refused to accept this gift, and devoted the whole of the proceeds to the building of an Infant School, which was sorely needed, and this is now a perpetual monument of his activity and zeal for the wellbeing of the Jews in Liverpool. A testimonial of a set of diamond studs and a ring was also presented to Mr. Hess, the Honorary Secretary of the Building Committee.

There are various gifts to the new synagogue that deserve to be recorded ; first a splendid *Almemar*, by Mr. David Lewis ; a marble pulpit by Mrs. Henrietta Braham, in memory of her late husband ; by Mrs. F. Samuel, a tablet of the Ten Commandments, also in memory of her late husband, and one of the most elaborately embroidered hangings by Mr. Morris Ranger, a drawing of which was depicted by the *Graphic*. Mr. R. H. Samuel presented two brazen candelabras ; Mr. Augustus S. Levy presented a valuable set of sacret vestments, together with a Scroll of the Law and rich congregational plate ; Mr. Ehrenbacher, Mr. John Cowan, Mr. Davidson, Mrs. D. Lewis and several others contributing to the sacred furniture of the building.

We have brought the principal events of the Old Hebrew Congregation to a close, and now revert to the New Congregation.

It is said, "Happy is the country that has no history." This may be applied to the Hope Place Congregation ; they are a quiet though flourishing community, having an income of about £1,000 a year. The services are ably conducted by their learned and talented minister, the Rev. Dr. Stern, and the congregants are ever ready to take part in any good work that concerns the community at large. The new congregation owe a deep debt of gratitude to two of their prominent members, Mr. Louis Davis and Mr. Joseph Harris, the former their representative at the Board of Deputies, who has acted for above a quarter of a century as honorary secretary, and has, by his energy and perseverance, led the congregation on to their path of success; whilst the latter gentleman, Mr. Joseph Harris, served as honorary Chazan for many years, thus enabling the community to relieve themselves of their heavy debt. Mr. Schönstadt and Mr. Saqui deserve honourable mention for the very efficient manner in which, during their years of wardenship, they introduced a spirit of decorum into the Divine service.

We shall now detail the numerous charities and institutions of the town. First, the school. This is a most successful institution, and has recently been much enlarged by the Infant School presented by Mr. Hoffnung, and still more recently by an additional room built and furnished at the joint expense of Messrs. Hoffnung, Ranger and Newgass. The institution is under Government Inspection and enjoys a grant of nearly £200. The schools are ably managed by a most efficient Board, the President being Mr. H. Samuel. Attached to the school are various prize funds, notably the Maria Behrend Fund, the Barned Prize, the Mozley Fund, the Esther Hoffnung Prize Fund, and the clothing fund founded by the late George Stankie, in which Mr. R. H. Samuel, the chairman, takes a great interest. There is also a soup fund for providing the children with food during the winter months. The sanitary arrangements are admirably cared for by Dr. Lewis, who gives much of his valuable time to the relief of the sick poor.

The oldest charitable society in the town is the Philanthropic Society for providing a sum of not less than 4s. per week to deserving poor during the winter months. It was founded in 1811 by Mr. Moses Samuel. The Ladies' Benevolent Institution was founded in 1849 by Mrs. B. Levy and Mrs. Jacobs, and the funds are devoted to providing poor Jewish women with medical aid and general assistance during their confinement. They hold a periodical ball, one of the most fashionable of the season. The one held in January last netted £600. The Provident Society, founded by the late Mr. Sussman Solomon, provides annuities for aged and deserving Jews above the age of 60. There is also attached to the Old Hebrew Congregation the Barned Annuity Fund, providing £20 per annum each for five decayed residents, as well as a coal and blanket fund, founded by the Mozley family. The Jewish young men have a Literary and Debating Society, where they meet for mutual instruction and discussion. Their meetings are held weekly at the Hebrew Schools, in Hope Place. The latest addition to the charitable institutions of the town is the Board of Guardians, which, being but in the first year of its existence, is only tentative, though it promises to be of much use in dispensing local charity. Within the last few months a series of almshouses were built and endowed by Mrs. Braham and the late Miss Eliza Jackson. These form six residences for aged widows and spinsters, besides giving each occupant annually a sum of £25.

Liverpool may be said to be the cradle of the Anglo-Jewish Association; this was first established as a branch of the Alliance in Paris in 1867, by Mr. B. L. Benas and Mr. Mark Samuel. Mr. B. L. Benas has been its President since the foundation, and has introduced to Liverpool, at large public meetings, the late Professor Waley, and recently the Baron Henry de Worms and other influential members of the London Council. There are few communities that have contained men reflecting greater credit to the Jews of England than Liverpool. Professor Sylvester, Dr. Van Oven, Dr. Behrend, Professor Marks, Serjeant Simon, M.P., and Professor Isaacs were at one period of their existence residents in the town; and Professor Leone Levi, whilst in Liverpool, was an observant member of our faith.

Mr. Samuel Montague, who takes a prominent interest in metropolitan Jewish affairs, is a type of that character so dear to English boys who owe their advancement to their own exertions, and, like all self-made men, is no doubt proud of the fact of having left Liverpool an obscure and unknown lad, and has won the distinguished privilege of participating in every charitable and communal object tending to the benefit of his coreligionists.

Without mentioning a special name, it is gratifying to know that in all the learned institutions—in the Literary and Philosophical Society, in the Historic Society, and in the Philomathic Society—our co-religionists are to be found taking a leading interest in their proceedings, and several valuable papers have been contributed to their volumes by Jews. In local politics, our race, although pursuing different shades of political opinions, has also come to the fore.

Mr. Charles Mozley occupied the position of Mayor of Liverpool in 1865. Mr. S. Moss has been a Member of the Select Vestry of the town for many years. Mr. B. L. Benas is Vice-President of the Constitutional Association for St. Peter's Ward, one of the largest and most important in the borough; and Mr. Charles Simpson Samuell is Deputy-Coroner for the town and district.

There is an ever increasing Jewish population in the town, and it may fairly be hoped that they will proceed for many years in their career of prosperity. There is always a difficulty in compiling the memorabilia of a town, district, or community. To include every item of local interest would cause the work to expand into a volume, and would not interest the general reader, so that the only option left the journalist is to sketch the salient outlines, which this record only professes to do. The narrative would, however, be incomplete without mentioning the prospective legacies which in due course will accrue to the revenues of the old congregation by the will of the late Mr. James Braham. This gentleman has bequeathed the sum of £30,000 to endow an English lectureship and a reader, also to provide annually a marriage portion to one of the three best girls in the Liverpool Jewish School—an interesting part of the provision being that the three best are to draw lots and the successful girl to be the recipient of the gift.

It is, we believe, of infinite benefit to the different communities to see themselves as others see them ; it stimulates them to further exertions when they are aware that public opinion appreciates their laudable endeavours, whilst their errors will be avoided when these are brought up in judgment against them by the cold and impartial criticism of history. Taking the two Liverpool Jewish congregations into brief survey, we can only repeat that we wish there were more like them in the United Kingdom. We propose in our next to narrate the early struggles for synagogue decorum in the Liverpool community.

As we have already narrated, the early settlers in Liverpool were of that class of co-religionists who, however excellent in their religious zeal for the faith of their forefathers, were not of the same high type of Jewish character as those "*preux chevaliers*" of Spain and Portugal who, in the words of the Rabbis, combined "religion with the ways of the world." From the records they have left behind, it seems they could neither speak German, Hebrew, nor English, but that their vocabulary was an admixture of all three languages. In their first law book we find such choice morsels as "the *baalbatim* must be assembled at an *asseefa*." This means in *loshon* English a "meeting," or Rov. dias.—this is in *loshon* English a majority. Hence a wall of demarcation separated them from the Christian inhabitants of the town ; the Jews had no interests beyond those of their shops and their synagogue; they were quite content to live unnoticed, and even courted obscurity. One of the early laws reads as follows : "If any of the children of our community have a dispute, be it in civil matters or otherwise, they shall not dare to bring this before the tribunal of the *Goyim* without the consent of the *Parnass* and elders for the time being, and if any one dare do so he shall be *poresh*, or excommunicated from the midst of his brethren."

They were not unwise who framed this enactment, as at those periods a Jew was looked upon in provincial England as an abnormal character, and as a being that ought to have no existence out of the pages of the Old Testament. The few Christians who were of a tolerant disposition at that period always had in their mind's eye, when thinking of the living Israelite, one old, decrepit and slouchy individual, with a long white beard reaching to his waist, leaning upon the arm of a young Jewish maiden. These were the only two types of Jews known to the outer world for many centuries, a Shylock and Jessica, and an Isaac of York and a Rebecca. The youthful, manly, vigorous Jew was an unknown character to the Christian of the former days. He could only typify the religion and the race as worn out and dying with a young and beautiful daughter to become the heritage of the Gentile. But things have vastly changed since " George the Third was King," and we can only praise the early desire of the Jews to do what little laundry work there existed within the precints of their own premises.

The synagogue of the first Liverpool Jews was their second home, the chief theme of their thoughts, and the highest object of their solicitude. To be an elder was like a step to the legislature, and to become a *Gabba*, or Parnass, was the crowning achievement of their desires. To do a little " chazonos " or chanting, seems to have been cultivated by every member of the community, and each endeavoured to outvie the other in the mode of rendering the weekly Haphtora, which was read to the congregation by the one called to the Maphtir. To act occasionally as " Baal Tephilah," or lay reader, was quite an enviable distinction, and, as a matter of course, every one read up for the part, which he at any moment might be called upon to perform. Thus a vivid interest was taken in all the minutiæ of Divine worship. No Piyut was too long, for every melody was criticised by a congregation of " dilletanti," and a good long service was keenly enjoyed by the worshippers.

But a change had necessarily to take place, owing to the force of circumstances. The original settlers had received their knowledge of Hebrew and religion in Germany and Poland, " where it was to the manner born " with them, whilst their children in Liverpool were both unable and unwilling to acquire the same proficiency in the sacred tongue. Unlike their parents, who could not identify themselves with anything British, the younger Jewish men and women felt themselves English, and their sympathies and tastes went entirely with the land of their birth. Hence a reaction took place, and they soon went to the other extreme. The younger members did not pause to consider that it was less the religion of their fathers than their German and Polish habits and errors of diction that required

to be improved. Faults of manner and peculiarity of dress were
ascribed by the rising youth to the Jewish religion, whilst the
very same defects could be found in any German or Polish immi-
grant of the lower ranks, whether he be a member of the Lutheran
faith or of the Catholic Church. They could not see, that as with
a kaleidoscope, if the figure is to be changed, it is not to be done
by breaking the instrument, and scattering the prisms, but rather
by shifting the position, that another and, perhaps, a more brilliant effect is produced.

Again, a number of young men emigrated to various colonies.
They left with little knowledge of Hebrew and religion, and
that little was entirely lost by their long isolation from Judaism.
Some of them returned with fortunes, but were perfectly ignorant
of everything connected with the Hebrew language or faith; and
living as they did among a semi-civilised population, it tended
neither to improve their manners nor to teach them to exercise a
spirit of forbearance towards the imperfections of the departing
generations, so that on their return, like the Vandal of old, they
endeavoured to destroy, indiscriminately, both that which was really
useful together with that which might be superfluous in the religious
customs of Judaism. From the struggle of conflicting opinions a
new state of affairs ensued. The Liverpool community at that
period might be divided into three camps. The first section was
intolerantly orthodox, and who would have deemed the sacrifice of
a line in the prayer book as rank heresy, while they looked upon
Jüdisch Deutsch as second only in sanctity to the sacred
tongue. The programme of the second section was gradual modi-
fication of the ritual adapted to the altered conditions of the state
of feeling among the Jews themselves, but always with the old
materials, and on the same lines. They had an ardent love for
their faith, and believed in its vitality as a powerful agent in the
spiritual regeneration of their co-religionists; they made every
sacrifice to educate the poorer classes, and there was no charitable
institution for which this section of the Jewish population was
not prepared to give both their time and services. They were
not only Jews by faith, but they took pains to identify themselves with the Jewish cause generally. The third division was
the Vandal element, who assumed to be more English than the
English themselves, who disliked everything Jewish, and merely
remained in its fold by reason of its being the only circle in which
they could rise to any importance. Not having sufficient culture
to shine elsewhere, they aspired to be shining lights among their
own co-religionists. They had nothing in common with their
brethren; in fact, they made an open boast of their ignorance of
the Hebrew language, and always indulged in a quiet sneer at the
Jews and everything Jewish.

The struggle now commenced between the different factions, and whole columns of the *Cup of Salvation*, a monthly publication issued in Liverpool some thirty years ago, of which we have spoken in a previous article, are directed against the insidious attacks of "these Hebrew pagans, who remain in the fold only to attack Judaism the more readily, and who have not the moral courage of the apostate who openly leaves it."

The secession of the Hope Place Congregation was the utter discomfiture of the "nihilistic" element. Those who would destroy the whole Jewish character of the ritual, abolish the Hebrew language, and reduce the religion to a species of Jewish Unitarianism, had to moderate their demands, and the party may now be said, with the exception of a few solitary remnants, to have died out.

The benefits which the moderate men of Liverpool have conferred upon the Jewish community are manifold. They introduced, long before this was adopted in metropolitan communities, an orderly system. They made the English sermon an integral portion of Divine worship, and in order to induce the fair sex to attend synagogue, they divided the early Sabbath service from the Musaph—the latter being commenced at 10.30, an hour suitable for all. The choir, one of the very best in Great Britain, led at the opening of the Musaph with the 92nd Psalm, and closed the service with the Adon Olam, this practice being afterwards adopted by the Bayswater congregation.

The mode of *Chazonos* was much modified, and instead of the perpetual chant of the older style, or the monotone of the Berkeley Street reform, a recitative was adopted with choral responses. The ministers do not enter the synagogue until the moment the service begins; nor do the worshippers divest themselves of their *Talysim* until the ministers all leave the holy edifice in procession; and so well is the discipline of the congregants maintained that not even on Yom Kippur evening, at the conclusion of the fast, is there now any semblance of hurry or confusion.

The Piyutim are nearly all extracted from the service, and there is only one representative Cohen, who utters the priestly benediction on the festivals; whilst the Chasan Torah and Chasan Bereshith on Simhhath Torah are always identified by the two ministers, none except the ministers or readers are allowed to perform any of the so-called Mitzvoth, such as opening the ark, elevating the Scrolls of the Law, or reading the Haphtorah. Again, the Parnassim box, so conspicuously placed in other synagogues in front of the Almemar, has been removed, and the railing round the ladies' gallery has been completely abolished. Indeed, whilst maintaining the old orthodox lines, the service in the Prince's

Road Synagogue is in many respects an improvement upon the Berkeley Street Synagogue. It is quite as decorous, much more attractive, and although there is no organ accompaniment, a full choir, concealed in a gallery constructed for the purpose, throws a volume of sound throughout the building in many respects with more melodious effect than with instrumental aid.

But order and decorum are not merely confined to the greater synagogue. The Hope Place congregation have managed their affairs equally well, and, if anything, the balance of religious fervour is in favour of the secession synagogue, and there is scarcely a desirable feature in public worship introduced in the old congregation but it is not immediately reproduced in the younger community. By means of their public spirit, the Jewish body in Liverpool have brought themselves prominently under the notice of their fellow-townsmen of other denominations, and they are treated by them in every respect with equality, and even deference.

Perhaps an unique feature in the annals of Great Britain was apparent on the Hospital Sunday of 1875, when the Mayor, Aldermen, and several of the Council, although of the Christian faith, attended divine service at the synagogue, the Mayor in his chain of office and in his state carriage with outriders; the municipal servants in gorgeous livery standing sentry at the doors of the sacred edifice, and both the Chief Magistrate and the Corporate officials expressed themselves much impressed with the beautiful service which is specially arranged every year for that day. The editors of the local press of every shade of political opinion are particularly respectful towards their Jewish townsmen, as we shall proceed to show in our next by extracts from various local journals.

There are some incidents in a community or a country that stand out so prominently that they dwarf everything anterior to them, and form a " Pharos " or beacon to subsequent generations.

Thus the Norman conquest is an indelible landmark of English history—everything dating from that event, or is related as prior to that occurrence. So with the Arabs, the Hegira is the period from which they really with fondness trace their history; they have no desire to go beyond that.

Subsequent Jewish residents in Liverpool will in a like manner date every event in their community from the building of their really magnificent synagogue. The previous history of their congregation will have been dwarfed into insignificance; indeed, as one of their able and talented town councillors, Mr. Picton, F.S.A., so tersely put it in an after-dinner speech : " One of the best proofs that could be afforded of the wonderful advance which had taken place, not only in the trade of the town, but in the liberality of those who carried it on, was found in the fact that the highest sum subscribed to the Seel Street building was 18 guineas, whereas that evening he had heard it announced that one gentleman had given £1,000. Therefore, as 18 guineas were to £1,000, so was the trade of Liverpool in 1807 to that in 1872."

To give an illustration of the difference in the status of the Jewish community we make an extract from *Porcupine* (a local journal) of Aug. 5th, 1865, and Sept. 5th, 1874 :—

Aug. 5th, 1865, reads : " The Seel Street Synagogue, in which the Jews of Liverpool have worshipped for some generations, is a small building, insignificant as to dimensions, but of some pretensions as to architectural character. It stands back from the pavement of the unattractive street in which it is situated, and is enclosed within iron railings; having no peculiarity by which the stranger may distinguish it from the Christian buildings around, except the Hebrew inscription above the entrance. The visitor whose piety or curiosity leads him to cross the threshold, finds himself in a small lobby or hall, with a snug room or closet for the accommodation of the doorkeeper on the left hand, and a staircase leading to the gallery on the right. The body of the synagogue is partly concealed from him by the hanging curtains which face the entrance ; and around this inner doorway may be found, at most periods of the service, a knot of young Jews sprucely dressed, and wearing the large black hats from which most classes of Christian lads have of late years been emancipated. Should the too reverential and incautious visitor, ignorant or forgetful of Hebrew usages, respectfully take off his hat as he passes through this modest vestibule, these younger sons of Abraham, though apparently somewhat lax about their own devotional observances, will speedily take him to task, and convince him that to uncover his head is not thought reverential here."

Sept. 1874, reads : " The consecration of the new Jewish synagogue, Prince's Road, on Thursday, was a very effective and impressive ceremony. Under any circumstances, and in almost any building, the services could not fail to be conducive to deep reflection upon things most solemn and sacred ; but in such a grand and glorious temple as the munificence and taste of the Old Hebrew Congregation of Liverpool, coupled with the marvellous skill and high culture of the architects—the Messrs. Audsley—have produced, there was everything to enhance the solemnity and beauty, combined with singularly expressive simplicity of the services. To those comparatively unacquainted with the rites and ceremonies of the Jewish religion, the scene which the well-filled and strikingly beautiful temple presented was in every sense imposing and remarkably suggestive. Prejudices against the ' ancient people ' must be strong indeed, and have got a tenacious grip upon the heart, if they did not slacken or give in sight of the glowing breadth of heartfelt charity, which the mingling of creeds and classes in the synagogue so eloquently implied. The gathering together of men of all shades of opinion in religion and politics upon such an occasion must act beneficially upon the whole community. And the address of the venerable Chief Rabbi, Dr. Adler, was well calculated to promote and extend feelings of true charity and goodwill. The banquet in the evening at the small Concert-room, which brought to a close this memorable day to the members of the Old Jewish Congregation, was distinguished by a display of skill in the arrangement and decoration of the tables, which was the subject of general remark. The speeches of Mr. Hoffnung, the President, were distinguished for fluency, good taste and high culture. His historical references were as apt and truthful as they were forcible and telling. Liverpool should certainly hear more of this highly-gifted gentleman, and the Old Hebrew Congregation are to be congratulated upon possessing such an able and brilliant member."

The following is an extract from a Conservative organ, the *Liverpool Courier*, of September 4th, 1874 :—

" The Jews, as a people, are loyal citizens of the state in which they dwell—certainly they are so in England. Their religion has no political bias, and all they ask is permission to practise their creed in peace and quiet ; nor is their religion of an aggressive turn—they rather discourage than seek proselytes, and it is no part of their ambition to convert the world to their belief. In social habits, too, they are orderly and self-reliant, and themselves bear burdens which other sects cast upon the State. Indeed, the Jews are more than an interesting people—they are in some respects an exemplary sect ; while, in no sense, is the prejudice against them founded in actual truth. Now they are not required to make sacrifices in their persons and goods; they are not despoiled of their property, banished, or maltreated, as were their forefathers ; but they still make voluntary sacrifices for their faith, which puts to the blush more pretentious sects. The synagogue, which was yesterday dedicated to the service of God, is a splendid monument of their liberality and their desire to make the temple worthy of its high destiny. The Jewish community is not a numerous one, and, contrary to common belief, it is not, as a rule, a wealthy one ; yet this small body has erected a Church, which, for splendour and richness, will compare with any other fane in Liverpool. Indeed, we doubt whether it has a local rival. Such magnificence and religious zeal deserve recognition, and we are sure the public of Liverpool will think well of a sect which at its own cost has raised the edifice. They, too, are naturally proud of the achievement."

The *Liverpool Daily Post*, the organ of the extreme Liberal party, thus expresses itself :—

"The first reflection on such a scene as that of yesterday is the the extent to which the Jews have advanced under favour of the age's enlightenment into the serene enjoyment of full religious liberty, and even full religious recognition. But, when we look closer, we see that it is not merely the Jews who have thus been benefited, but that every form of religion has, in turn, been subjected to persecutions from which it has in its turn been freed, and to prejudices out of which increasing intelligence has taken the sting. There is not a sect in England or in Europe, of more than mushroom growth, which has not passed through the fire of persecution and the frettings of social disparagement. Toleration is a late discovery, and it has been but slowly perfected. The world waited until our own time to learn the lesson in which yesterday's interesting proceedings showed such proficiency amongst religionists of almost every nature. And what is the result ? Is truth less firmly held ? Has religious zeal on behalf of our own Church evaporated in vague latitudinarian sentimentality ? Let the sturdy sermon of the Chief Rabbi answer the first question. Let the fine edifice in Prince's Road and the munificent contributions offered yesterday to make it still grander, reply to the second. Nor need we fear that any of the Christian sympathizers present at its dedication will show less zeal for the faith into which they have progressed from the elements of Judaism because they are capable of delighting in the great truths and the great emotions which still live in Judaic forms. It is now perceived at last that perfect toleration carried to the extent of brotherly sentiment amongst all who love and practise religion is the best protector for the liberty and felicity of all, and the surest guarantee that whatever is good and true in any religion shall have its due effect in freely attracting to itself those of other ways of thinking. What more can any desire who believe that they hold the truth ? The effects of similar free principles in politics, and the honourable eminence of the Jews as tests and standards of the freedom of the various nations of the world, have seldom been so eloquently elucidated as in the really eloquent and pregnant speeches of Mr. Hoffnung at the banquet by which yesterday's consecration service was followed. The proceedings of the whole day were of such high significance as illustrative of religious zeal, public spirit, and the progress of the age in freedom and justice, as to deserve a distinct and notable place in our annals."

Let the *Liverpool Mercury* of Feb. 11th, 1874, give its own *resumé* of the history of the glorious bazaar :—

" Fancy fairs in aid of funds for the promotion of religious or benevolent object are of frequent occurrence amongst the Catholic and Protestant portions of the community ; but a Hebrew Ladies' Bazaar is something perfectly unique in England.   In America two or three such entertainments have taken place with great success, and large sums of money have been raised in furtherance of the special objects for which the bazaars were held.   The bazaar opened yesterday in St. George's Hall, with a view to assist in defraying the cost of erecting the Jewish synagogue in Princes Road in this town, was, however, the first of its kind in this kingdom, and was invested with more than ordinary interest.   At first only a sale of fancy work on a small scale was contemplated, but the contributions grew into such proportions that it was. found necessary to adopt some other means of disposing of the productions of the Hebrew ladies, and this bazaar was accordingly resolved on. The ladies, however, could only prepare the plain or fancy work which was to be disposed of, and then sell it to the best advantage. It needed some well-disciplined business man to take the management of the whole affair, and this gentleman was found in the person of Mr. Abraham Hoffnung, a merchant of this town, to whose indefatigable labours, in conjunction with those of others, members of the Hebrew community, viz., Messrs. Augustus S. Levy, B. L. Benas, S. Y. Hess, L. S. Cohen, and Geo. Behrend, the success of the bazaar is mainly attributable.   But its interest was by no means of a local character.   Contributions of various kinds were sent from different parts of the United Kingdom, from the Continent, and even from America, foremost among the leading members of the Hebrew community who interested themselves in the bazaar being the Baroness Lionel de Rothschild, who kindly accepted the office of patroness, and would have been present but for the death of a near relative.   The Baroness, however, expressed her sympathy with the movement by sending several valuable contributions to the bazaar.   Seldom has St. George's Hall presented a more beautiful appearance than it wore yesterday morning, when the fancy fair was formally opened."

We now proceed to draw this series of articles to a close, and we cannot do so without remarking the contrast between the mode of conducting communal meetings in Liverpool with other provincial towns, and even the metropolis.   There is a method, a discipline, and a certain business-like air in all their proceedings, unlike the " talkee," " talkee," to which we are accustomed in London and some provincial Jewish bodies.   This is mainly owing to the general contact of the Jews of Liverpool with local matters not immediately concerning their own sect, and more especially to the fact that the later residents are men of superior culture, and have, in many instances, received a college training. These do not, as did the Jews in former days, isolate themselves from their community, but act not only *for* their co-religionists, but *with* their brethren in faith. If the Jews of Liverpool do not fall back into the provincialisms and wranglings of the early part of the century, but, on the contrary, keep up the progress they have made during the last decade, they will undoubtedly remain "a model Jewish community of Great Britain."